Word 365
Styles and Breaks

EASY WORD 365 ESSENTIALS - BOOK 5

M.L. HUMPHREY

CONTENTS

Introduction

This book is part of the *Easy Word 365 Essentials* series of titles. These are targeted titles that are excerpted from the main *Word 365 Essentials* series and are focused on one specific topic.

If you want a more general introduction to Word, then you should check out the *Word 365 Essentials* titles instead. In this case, *Intermediate Word 365* which covers not only styles and breaks but track changes, multilevel lists, tables, and more.

But if all you want to learn is how to use styles and breaks in Word, then this is the book for you.

Styles

If you're going to do any formatting in Word, using styles will save you a tremendous amount of time and effort.

For example, the first print books I ever formatted I used Word. And I was able to set up three styles that I could use, one for the chapter names, one for the first paragraph of a chapter or section, and one for all other paragraphs. It was then a very simple matter to apply the "all other paragraphs" format to my entire document and then go through and for each chapter header and each first paragraph in a chapter or section apply the other formats.

That easily let me create a document with consistent formatting throughout.

A style has the font, font size, color, paragraph spacing, paragraph indent, etc. all built in, so you don't have to keep changing those settings. It's much better at ensuring consistency of appearance than trying to format your paragraphs manually. And much easier to apply than the Format Painter option.

Also, you can create shortcuts for your styles so that you don't even have to use your mouse, you can just use your keyboard shortcut to apply each style.

Alright. Let's walk through how to use them now.

Styles are located in the Styles section of the Home tab:

The number of styles that are visible by default will depend on your screen size, but usually it will be a handful or so. There is a downward-pointing arrow on the right-hand side of that listing (see the screenshot above) that you can click on to expand the list of styles. If you do so, it will look something like this:

in Excel. (If not, check out one of those books).

Those are all of the default styles that Word uses. Each one is formatted to show a bit of what that style will look like if applied to your text.

When I'm drafting a document like this one, I usually have my paragraphs use the Normal style and my chapters use the Heading 1 style. I then change the styles when I'm done and ready to format.

The Normal style will be applied to your text by default so you don't have to do anything to use it. But the Heading 1 style does have to be applied.

To apply a style to your text, click onto that paragraph or line of text. (You don't have to select all of the text, just click onto some portion of that paragraph or line of text.) Next, click on the style you want from the Style listing in the Styles section of the Home tab.

The Normal and Heading styles can also be applied using a control shortcut. Ctrl + Shift + N will apply the Normal style. Ctrl + Alt + 1 will apply Heading 1, Ctrl + Alt + 2 will apply Heading 2, and Ctrl + Alt + 3 will apply Heading 3.

If you use the Heading styles, Word will also show any text with those styles applied in your Navigation pane on the left-hand side under the Headings view. Here you can see my chapter names, Introduction, Terminology, Shortcuts, etc. from *Excel Tips and Tricks*, all of which were formatted using the Heading 1 style:

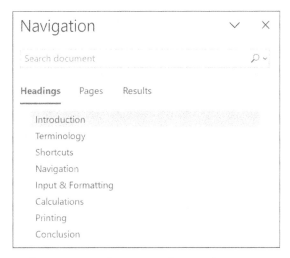

Click on each of those entries to go to that part of your document.

You can also left-click and drag one of those entries in that list to move the entire section to a new location in your document. The text that moves will be all text from that header through to the next text in the document that has that same heading style or a higher-level heading style.

Meaning, that if I have applied the Heading 1 style to all of my chapter titles and I left-click and drag one of my chapter titles to a new location in the list, that will move that entire chapter to the new location. But it will leave all subsequent chapters where they are.

Here, for example, I dragged Conclusion to the top above Introduction, which you can see on the left-hand-side listing. You can also see by looking at the document that all text from the chapter moved, too:

Here is an example where I've applied the Heading 2 style to the chapter sub-sections, Pin a File and Navigate Between Worksheets:

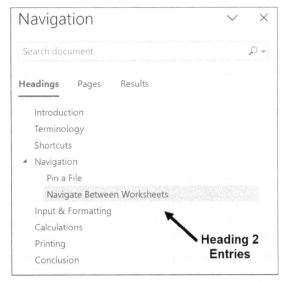

If I click and drag one of the Heading 2 entries, all text between that entry and the next listed heading will move. So if I move Pin a File, all text from there to Navigate Between Worksheets will move. But if I move Navigate Between Worksheets, all text from there to the next chapter, Input & Formatting, will move.

I know that sounds very complex, but if you need to do this, the best way to learn is to try it out and see what happens. I very rarely need to click and drag to move an entire section of my document, but it does sometimes happen. If the idea of doing so using the Headings listing scares you, there's always cut and paste.

Also, when you use a Heading level, like I did here with Heading 2, Word will automatically make the next heading level, in this case, Heading 3, available in the Styles section.

When you use the heading styles in your document, that also allows you to collapse those sections so the text under that heading is hidden, like I've done here for Pin a File:

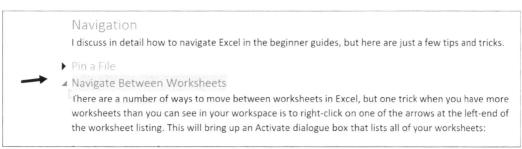

You still have the heading, but all of the text is hidden. When a section is collapsed like that, the black arrow to the left of the heading will be visible. Click on that to expand the section once more.

To collapse a section, you need to hold your mouse over the header to make that blue arrow appear on the left-hand side like I've done above for Navigate Between Worksheets. Click on that arrow to collapse the section and hide the text.

Headings are useful when drafting a large document, but the default Word styles are usually not what I want to use for my final document, so once I'm done I need to create custom styles or apply styles from another document.

Let's walk through how to do that now.

First off, I'm not a fan of messing with the default styles. So I try to leave Normal and the Headings alone. I won't directly modify those if I can avoid it.

Instead, what I do is I take a paragraph and I modify it so that it's formatted the way I want.

(If I have another document that is already formatted properly I will use the Format Painter from the Clipboard section of the Home tab to bring in that formatting for me. Sometimes that also brings in a style name, too, and I don't have to do the rest of these steps to create a new style, I can just apply it where needed. But assuming it doesn't…)

Next, once my paragraph is formatted the way I want, I expand the Styles section and click on the option to Create a Style. That brings up the Create New Style From Formatting dialogue box:

Create New Style from Formatting ? ✕

Name:

Style1

Paragraph style preview:

Style1

OK Modify… Cancel

I change the name of the style to something that I'll remember and then click OK. That adds that style as an option in the Styles section of the Home tab:

I can then click on that option to format any other paragraph in my document using that style. (We'll talk in a moment about how to do this quickly.)

If you want there to be a keyboard shortcut for that style, right-click on the style in the Styles section and choose Modify from the dropdown menu. That will open the Modify Style dialogue box. At the bottom of that dialogue box is a dropdown menu that says Format. Click on that to see a list of choices. The one you want is Shortcut Key:

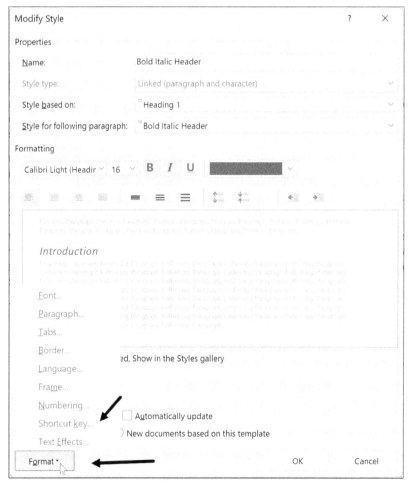

That will open a Customize Keyboard dialogue box where you can click into the Press New Shortcut Key field. Use the shortcut key combination you want and Word will populate it in that field. But watch out that the shortcut you come up with isn't already in use elsewhere. (Word will tell you if it is.)

Here I've assigned Ctrl + } to this style. Word shows that and also shows that it is currently not assigned to any other task:

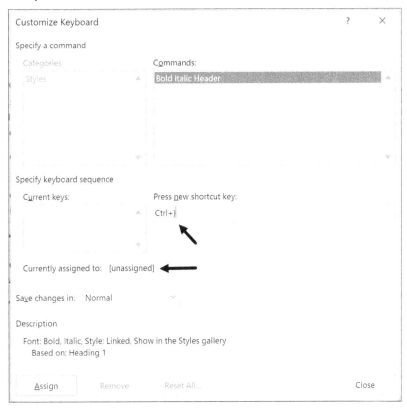

If I want to keep that as my shortcut I can then click on Assign and when I need that format I can apply it to any text in my document using the shortcut instead of having to go to the Style section up top. (It can save time to do this if you're applying styles as you move through a document, because a keyboard shortcut uses the keyboard whereas accessing the menus up top usually requires going to the mouse or trackpad.)

Often, though, what I do is I swap out all of my Normal-formatted paragraphs for paragraphs formatted in my custom style all at once. To do this, right-click on the Normal style option and choose Select All:

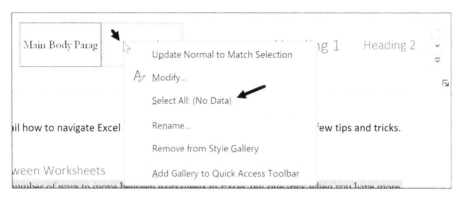

That will select all of the text in the document that uses the Normal style. Like this:

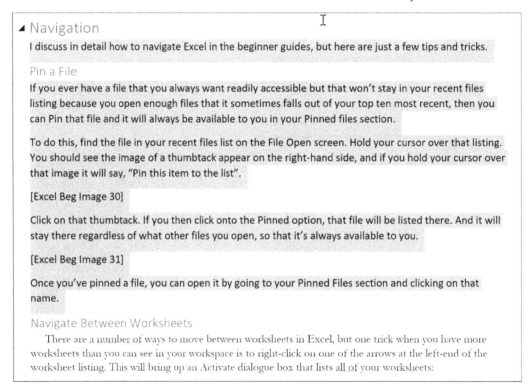

To change all of those Normal-style text entries over to a different style, select the new style from the Styles section. And done:

Navigation

I discuss in detail how to navigate Excel in the beginner guides, but here are just a few tips and tricks.

Pin a File

If you ever have a file that you always want readily accessible but that won't stay in your recent files listing because you open enough files that it sometimes falls out of your top ten most recent, then you can Pin that file and it will always be available to you in your Pinned files section.

To do this, find the file in your recent files list on the File Open screen. Hold your cursor over that listing. You should see the image of a thumbtack appear on the right-hand side, and if you hold your cursor over that image it will say, "Pin this item to the list".

[Excel Beg Image 30]

Click on that thumbtack. If you then click onto the Pinned option, that file will be listed there. And it will stay there regardless of what other files you open, so that it's always available to you.

[Excel Beg Image 31]

Once you've pinned a file, you can open it by going to your Pinned Files section and clicking on that name.

Navigate Between Worksheets

There are a number of ways to move between worksheets in Excel, but one trick when you have more worksheets than you can see in your workspace is to right-click on one of the arrows at the left-end of the worksheet listing. This will bring up an Activate dialogue box that lists all of your worksheets:

It only took about five seconds for Word to apply my new style to all of the paragraphs in my document that had used the Normal style previously. I could do the same for the Heading 1 and Heading 2 styles and then create a first paragraph style that uses a control shortcut and go through and manually apply that one.

A very easy way to format a document.

If you realize that your text style is not formatted the way you want, edit one paragraph of text that uses that style and then right-click on the style name at the top of the workspace and choose Update [Style Name] to Match Selection.

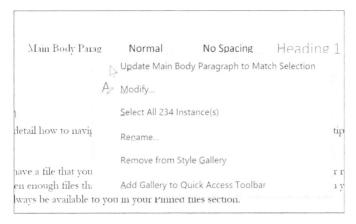

That will change all text entries in your document that use that style.

I find that easier than right-clicking on the style and choosing the Modify option which will open a Modify Style dialogue box where you can change any text or paragraph settings. It works, but it's easier for me to use the Paragraph and Font sections of the Home tab to modify a paragraph instead and then apply my changes that way.

Clicking on the expansion arrow for Styles will open a Styles floating task pane. You can click on Options there to open the Style Pane Options dialogue box which lets you control which styles are shown in the menu as well as a few other settings:

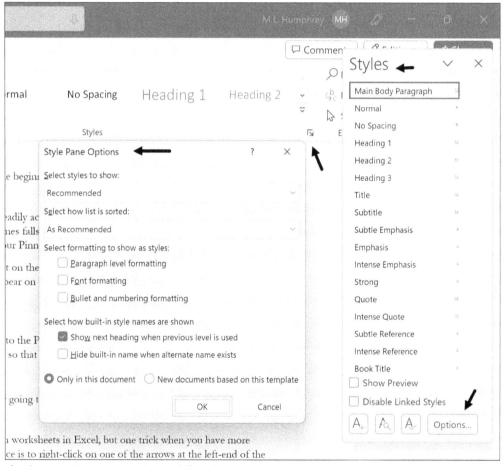

One final note. Every once in a while when I'm working with Heading 1 styles, Word will try to apply them to the paragraph above the chapter name. It's pretty obvious when it happens because you can see the text of that paragraph in the Headings section of the Navigation pane. If that ever happens to you, go to that paragraph, use Enter at the end of the paragraph and then apply the Normal style to it. The chapter name should keep the Heading 1 format, but it won't apply to that paragraph anymore.

And that's it. Pretty simple, but incredibly powerful. You should always use styles that incorporate paragraph formatting and indents instead of trying to use Enters, spaces, and the Tab key to format your text. Trust me on this.

Page Breaks

It can be tempting to use Enter to move text to the next page when that's needed. Don't. As I've mentioned before and I'll mention again, manually trying to force formatting onto your text is a very, very bad idea. It creates a lot of unnecessary work and is very prone to breaking or having inconsistencies. One little change somewhere in your document and suddenly everything is off.

The way to move text to the next page and not have all those issues is to use a Page Break. To insert one, go to the point in your document where you want to insert the break and then go to the Pages section of the Insert tab and click on Page Break:

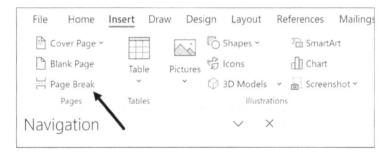

That will automatically move your cursor down to the next page in your document.

By default your page breaks in your document will not be visible. But if you click on the Show/Hide paragraph marks option in the Paragraph section of the Home tab, you can make them visible:

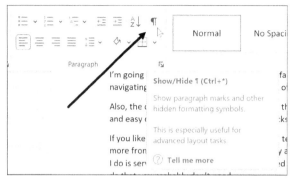

Here is an example of what that looks like:

In this case, the page break is on its own line. Sometimes that can be a problem because it forces a blank page that you don't want. If it is, you can click onto the line above and use Delete to bring the page break up to the last line of text.

If the last line of text is really long, sometimes you'll only see part of the text that identifies a page break:

To remove a page break, just treat it like any other text or paragraph mark and either use Delete or Backspace, depending on where you are relative to the break.

You can also find a page break option in the Page Setup section of the Layout tab under the Breaks dropdown menu:

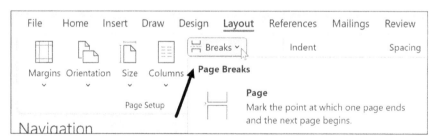

As I mentioned in *Word 365 for Beginners*, Page Break is actually a task that I add to my Quick Access Toolbar so that I don't have to go searching for it since I use it often enough and it's not on the Home tab.

Okay. Now let's discuss section breaks, which can also be found in that Breaks dropdown menu.

Section Breaks

Page breaks simply push text to the next page, but all of the formatting, document size, etc. remains the same. Section breaks, on the other hand, let you create different sections of your document that are formatted in different ways.

When might you need this?

If you are writing a report that has appendices that are landscape orientation instead of portrait orientation, you can achieve this in one single document by using section breaks between the main report and your appendices.

When I used to format print books using Word, I would use section breaks to have different headers and footers in different parts of my book.

So, for example, in the print version of this book you will see that the header for each chapter uses that chapter's name and that there is no header on the page that starts each chapter. The way to achieve that is to have different sections for each chapter.

Another place where that needs to happen is when you have a book that has all chapters starting on the right-hand page which sometimes requires a blank left-hand page. That can only be achieved if the blank page has different headers and footers compared to the other pages in the book.

Also, different sections are needed for any front matter, like tables of contents, which usually have separate page numbering from the main portion of the document.

* * *

Now that you understand what section breaks can be used for, let's look at your available options, which can be found in the Breaks dropdown in the Page Setup section of the Layout tab:

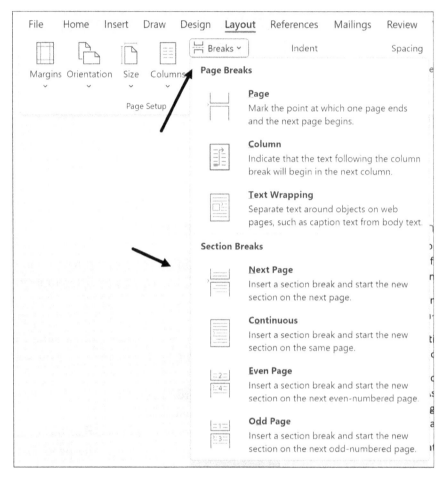

You have four choices there: Next Page, Continuous, Even Page, and Odd Page.

Continuous means that the break will happen on that same page. This could be used for a scenario where you have a single column of text at the top of the page and then multiple columns later in the page. Like this:

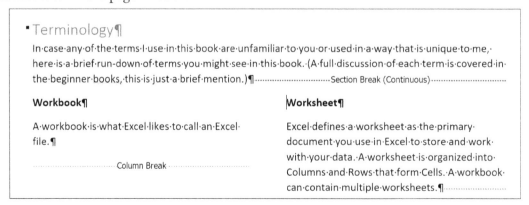

You can see here (maybe) that the first paragraph of that Terminology chapter is a single column. But then below that I have one column with the definition of Workbook next to another column with the definition for Worksheet. There is a Continuous Section Break between that first paragraph and the two definition columns.

When I selected that text and applied two-column formatting to it, Word automatically inserted the Section Break for me, which was nice, but I could have manually inserted it as well. (We'll come back to this more in the next chapter when we cover columns.)

The other three options, Next Page, Even Page, and Odd Page are all options that start a new section on another page. Just as their names imply, that other page is either the next one available, the next even-numbered page, or the next odd-numbered page.

For Even Page and Odd Page, Word will insert a blank page in between if needed.

Now, a warning here. I found in older versions of Word that when I tried to use the Odd Page Break, Word would accurately insert that particular section break, but it would somehow remove my previous odd-page section breaks from my document and turn them into next-page breaks instead.

I no longer use Word for book formatting and I wasn't able to replicate that issue today, so it may be fixed in Word 365 as of January 2023, but in case it isn't, Next Page Breaks always work. They just require a little extra effort if you're trying to have a blank page in there.

What I recommend, and you should do this anyway, is to be sure to check through your entire document when you're done and make sure that everything looks the way you want it. Okay.

Let's walk through this with an actual document that has headers and footers.

First, let's revisit the Headers & Footers Options section. As a reminder, you can add a header and/or footer to a document using the Header & Footer section of the Insert tab. When you do so, a Header & Footer tab will appear and in the Options section of that tab there will be three checkboxes:

Different First Page is what you need to use when the first page of your document or your section should have a different header and/or footer than the other pages.

Different Odd & Even Pages is what allows you to have different text on the left-hand page and the right-hand page, like in a book where you have author name on one side and book title or chapter title on the other.

Here, I've set it up so that there is no header on the first page, consistent page numbering on the bottom of all pages, and then the even-numbered pages have an author name and the odd-numbered pages have a book title in the header.

To get this to work, I had to add the page numbering to the first page, first even-numbered page, and first odd-numbered page separately.

I zoomed my document to 50% so we can see six pages at once:

It may be hard to see, but the top of that first page is blank. On the next page, in the header we have the author name. On the next one after that, in the header we have the book title. And then you can see for the next three pages how those alternate in the header between author name and title. Each page where you can see the footer has a page number that goes up by one with each page.

Problem is, that second page is the start of a new chapter, so the header should be blank. Same with the fourth page and sixth page that we can see.

To fix this, each of those pages needs to be the start of a new section.

It is a best practice when adding section breaks to start on page 1 and then work your way through the document and add those breaks as you go. The reason to do this is because as you add breaks the page numbers will shift and that may impact what kind of break you use on later chapters.

Theoretically, if you're using odd-numbered or even-numbered page breaks it won't matter, but for me I prefer to assume I'll have issues and do what I can to avoid them up front.

So I start by going to page 1 and replacing that Page Break with an Odd Page Section Break.

(Be careful that when you replace a Page Break with a Section Break, that you replace it, not add to it. The first time I did this, I highlighted Page Break and then inserted the Section

Break and it kept the Page Break and inserted the Section Break before it. I had to delete the Page Break first and then add the Section Break to get it to work.)

You can see here that now my "second" page also does not have a header, which is what we wanted:

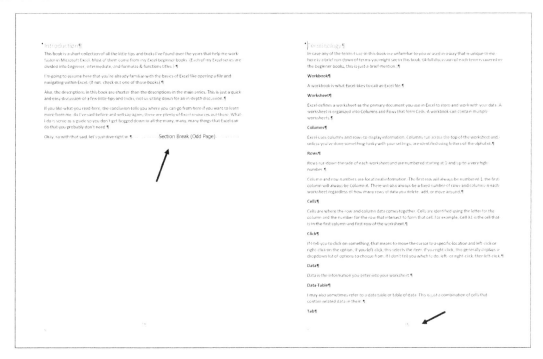

But I want to highlight something here that may be hard to see. That "second" page is actually the third page of the document. Because I used an Odd Page Section Break, Word, behind the scenes, has added a blank page between these two chapters. But it does not show on the screen. Nor does it show in Print Preview.

That blank page will only show up when the document is printed or generated as a PDF. You have to watch out for this because it is not intuitive to realize that there is a page that exists there but is not visible. Here is what that looks like when generated as a PDF:

I can now walk through the rest of my document and replace my page breaks with section breaks. I want to have each chapter start on an odd-numbered page, so I will use the Odd Page Section Break.

Word carries through the header and footer settings from the original document, so each new chapter has a blank first page header and then uses the author name and book title on the even- and odd-numbered pages, respectively. Each page is also numbered at the bottom.

For this book here, as written, that would be the end of it. But let's change things up a bit. I combined a few of my chapters so I'd have enough pages in each chapter to see the book title at the top of the page. Here are six pages from the middle of the book across two "chapters":

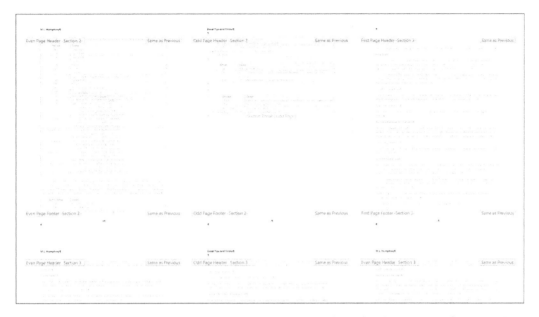

The headers and footers right now in these sections are linked. That means that any change I make to any of those headers or footers will carry over between the sections. For example, I just bolded the text in the headers for those first two pages and that bolding carried over to the bottom three pages.

But if you're trying to use different text at the top of a page for a section, you don't want that. The way to unlink your sections is to go to the Navigation section of the Header & Footer tab and unselect the Link to Previous option.

This is selected by default. Click into the second of the linked headers or footers first before you choose to unlink a header or footer since the option is to link to *previous*. Once you've unlinked your section from the prior section, you can edit the header or footer and it will not impact the prior section's header or footer.

If you are transitioning between front matter, like a table of contents, to the main body of your document or from the main body of your document to a standalone appendix, or using your chapter names for the header text, then you will need to do this.

I often find that I forget about this and make a change and then have to go back and unlink sections and then fix the one I inadvertently changed.

In my experience, working with section breaks and different headers and footers between those sections can take a little bit of trial and error to get everything to work properly. This is usually more about figuring out what should or should not be linked and making changes where they need to be made, but sometimes it seems to me that Word is more prone to do weird things the more complex your document becomes. So, don't get discouraged. Just fix things as they break and sometimes maybe find a simpler option (like a Next Page break instead of an Odd or Even Page break.)

Columns and Column Breaks

Since we just touched on it briefly above, I'm going to take a quick minute here and tell you how to change your document so that it has multiple columns of text on a single page.

First step, select your text that you want to place into multiple columns. Next, go to the Page Setup section of the Layout tab and click on the dropdown arrow below Columns.

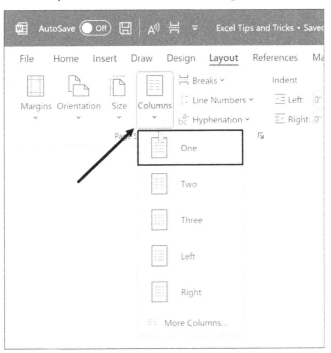

Choose your desired number of columns from the dropdown, which gives the option of one, two, or three columns as well as an option that has a skinnier left or right column next to a larger column.

If none of those options work for you, click on the More Columns option to bring up the Columns dialogue box:

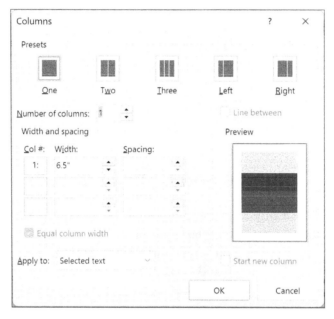

The dialogue box has those same options, but it also lets you specify different column widths for each column if you want.

You can also put a line between your columns if you want, like I've done here:

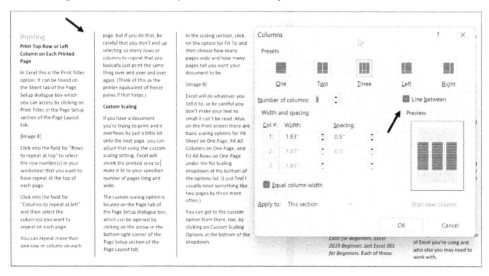

When you apply columns to a text selection, the default is for Word to spread that text evenly across the desired number of columns. Like so:

Workbook¶

A·workbook·is·what·Excel· likes·to·call·an·Excel·file.¶

Worksheet¶

Excel·defines·a·worksheet·as· the·primary·document·you· use·in·Excel·to·store·and· work·with·your·data.·A· worksheet·is·organized·into· Columns·and·Rows·that·form· Cells.·A·workbook·can· contain·multiple·worksheets.¶

Columns¶

Excel·uses·columns·and·rows· to·display·information.· Columns·run·across·the·top· of·the·worksheet·and,·unless· you've·done·something·funky· with·your·settings,·are· identified·using·letters·of·the· alphabet.¶

Rows¶

Rows·run·down·the·side·of· each·worksheet·and·are· numbered·starting·at·1·and· up·to·a·very·high·number.¶

Column·and·row·numbers· are·locational·information.·

The·first·row·will·always·be· numbered·1,·the·first·column· will·always·be·Column·A.· There·will·also·always·be·a· fixed·number·of·rows·and· columns·in·each·worksheet· regardless·of·how·many·rows· of·data·you·delete,·add,·or· move·around.¶

Cells¶

Cells·are·where·the·row·and· column·data·comes·together.· Cells·are·identified·using·the· letter·for·the·column·and·the· number·for·the·row·that· intersect·to·form·that·cell.· For·example,·Cell·A1·is·the· cell·that·is·in·the·first·column· and·first·row·of·the· worksheet.¶

Click¶

If·I·tell·you·to·click·on· something,·that·means·to· move·the·cursor·to·a·specific· location·and·left-click·or· right-click·on·the·option.·If· you·left-click,·this·selects·the· item.·If·you·right-click,·this· generally·displays·a· dropdown·list·of·options·to·

choose·from.·If·I·don't·tell· you·which·to·do,·left-·or· right-click,·then·left-click.¶

Data¶

Data·is·the·information·you· enter·into·your·worksheet.¶

Data·Table¶

I·may·also·sometimes·refer· to·a·data·table·or·table·of· data.·This·is·just·a· combination·of·cells·that· contain·related·data·in·them.¶

Tab¶

Tabs·are·the·options·you· have·to·choose·from·at·the· top·of·the·workspace.·The· default·tab·names·are·File,· Home,·Insert,·Page·Layout,· Formulas,·Data,·Review,· View,·and·Help.·But·there·are· certain·times·when· additional·tabs·will·appear,· for·example,·when·you· create·a·pivot·table·or·a· chart.¶

(This·should·not·be·confused· with·the·Tab·key·which·can· be·used·to·move·across· cells.)¶·Section·Break·(Continuous)·

Here I've taken a text selection and placed the text into three columns. If you read the entries, the text goes all the way down the first column and then continues to the second and then to the third. But because it's a selection, the amount of text in each column is about the same.

If you apply columns to an entire document instead, it will fill the first column on the page and then move on to the next column and then the next. In situations where there isn't enough text to fill the page you end up with something like this:

See how on the left-hand page there are only two columns with text in them and how on the right-hand page there are only two lines of text in the last column but the other two columns are full?

To balance the text across a page, click at the very end of the text on that page and then apply a Continuous Section Break. (Page Setup section of the Layout tab, Breaks dropdown, Section Breaks, Continuous.) Your result will look something like this:

As mentioned above in the chapter on section breaks, if you add columns to a selection of text in your document, Word will automatically add the Continuous Section Breaks for you at the start and at the end of the selection.

Sometimes where the text falls naturally is not going to be what you want. Like here:

Workbook	Excel defines a worksheet as the primary document you use in Excel to store and work with your data. A worksheet is organized into Columns and Rows that form Cells. A workbook can contain multiple worksheets.
A workbook is what Excel likes to call an Excel file.	
Worksheet	

I put these entries into two columns, but the problem is that "Worksheet" naturally falls at the bottom of the left-hand column when it would be better placed at the top of the right-hand column.

You can force the text to break at a different point by inserting a Column Break. To do so, click where you need the break and then go to the Page Setup section of the Layout Tab and choose Column from the Breaks dropdown menu.

Much better:

Workbook	**Worksheet**
A workbook is what Excel likes to call an Excel file.	Excel defines a worksheet as the primary document you use in Excel to store and work with your data. A worksheet is organized into Columns and Rows that form Cells. A workbook can contain multiple worksheets.

Appendix A: Basic Terminology Recap

These terms were covered in detail in *Word 365 for Beginners*. This is just meant as a refresher.

Tab

When I refer to a tab, I am referring to the menu options at the top of the screen. The tab options that are available by default are File, Home, Insert, Draw, Design, Layout, References, Mailings, Review, View, and Help, but for certain tasks additional tabs will appear.

Click

If I tell you to click on something, that means to move your cursor over to that location and then either right-click or left-click. If I don't say which to do, left-click.

Left-Click / Right-Click

A left-click is generally for selecting something and involves using the left-hand side of your mouse or bottom left-hand corner of your trackpad. A right-click is generally for opening a dropdown menu and involves using the right-hand side of your mouse or bottom right-hand corner of your trackpad.

Left-Click and Drag

Left-click and drag means to left-click and then hold that left-click as you move your mouse.

Dropdown Menu

A dropdown menu is a list of choices that you can view by right-clicking in a specific spot or clicking on an arrow next to or below one of the available choices under the tabs up top. Depending on where you are in the workspace, a dropdown menu may actually drop upward from that spot.

Expansion Arrow

In the bottom right corner of some of the sections under the tabs in the top menu you will see an arrow, which I refer to as an expansion arrow. Clicking on an expansion arrow will usually open a dialogue box or task pane and is often the way to see the largest number of options.

Dialogue Box

A dialogue box is a pop-up box that will open on top of your workspace and will usually include the largest number of choices for that particular setting or task.

Scroll Bar

Scroll bars appear when there are more options than can appear on the screen or when your document is longer than will show on the screen. They can be used to move through the remainder of the choices or document.

Task Pane

A task pane is a set of additional options that will appear to the sides or even below the main workspace. The Navigation pane is by default visible on the left-hand side of the workspace. You can close a task pane by clicking on the X in the top right corner of the pane.

Control Shortcuts

Control shortcuts are shortcuts that let you perform certain tasks in Word. I will write them as Ctrl + and then a character. That means to hold down both the Ctrl key and that character. So Ctrl + C means hold down Ctrl and C, which will let you copy your selection. Even though I will write each shortcut using a capital letter it doesn't have to be the capitalized version to work.

About the Author

M.L. Humphrey is a former stockbroker with a degree in Economics from Stanford and an MBA from Wharton who has spent close to twenty years as a regulator and consultant in the financial services industry.

You can reach M.L. at mlhumphreywriter@gmail.com or at mlhumphrey.com.

www.ingramcontent.com/pod-product-compliance
Lightning Source LLC
Chambersburg PA
CBHW060512060326
40689CB00020B/4710